⊕ AN OBSE1

Making Cloth

Tailoring Techniques

Gerald Marshall Hall

Illustrations by Coral Mula

FREDERICK WARNE

Published by Frederick Warne (Publishers) Ltd London, 1984
Text © Gerald Marshall Hall, 1984.
Illustrations © Frederick Warne (Publishers) Ltd, 1984

For my students, past, present and future

Imperial and metric measurements are used throughout this book.
Choose either the metric or the imperial system and stick to it throughout
each project—changing from one system to another will lead to
inaccuracy and mistakes.

ISBN 0 7232 3238 5

Typeset and Printed by BAS Printers Limited
Over Wallop, Hampshire

Contents

	Page
Introduction	5

Phase 1. Equipment   7

Hand-sewing needles. Sewing-machine needles. Tacking threads. Tailor's thimble. Hand-sewing threads. Beeswax. Dressmaker's pins. Scissors. Tailor's chalk. Wax chalk. Tracing wheel. Dressmaker's carbon tracing paper. Pencils. Pens. Pattern making paper. Pressing equipment

Phase 2. Choice—fabrics, patterns, linings and interfacings   18

Phase 3. Patterns   23

Proving the pattern. Multi-size patterns. Pattern conservation. Mixing pattern sizes. Alterations to paper patterns

Phase 4. Cutting out   30

Laying out fabric. Laying on the pattern. Cutting out

Phase 5. Marking techniques   34

Thread marking—close version. Thread marking—open version. Using thread marks—on patterns without seam allowances. Using thread marks—on patterns with seam allowances. Marking placement lines

Phase 6. Assembly   38

Stage one—the basic shell. Stage two—interfacing insertion. Stage three—covering the interfacing; making the pockets. Stage four—finishing. Twist button-holes. Variations on a theme

Introduction

Everything was finished except just one single cherry-coloured button-hole, and where that button-hole was wanting there was pinned a scrap of paper with these words—in little teeny weeny writing—NO MORE TWIST

Any craftsman or craftswoman reading *The Tailor of Gloucester* by Beatrix Potter cannot fail to be moved by the loving tender care those little mice gave when making those button-holes.

Tailoring, like any other craft that uses malleable materials, follows a sequence of events in which the tailor keeps a firm but kindly hand on the reins, always steady but forever guiding the project forwards. *Tailoring Techniques* deals with the softer but not necessarily easier aspect of tailoring women's clothes. I have chosen a ladies' jacket as the main project because most of the problems encountered and the techniques applied in making other tailored garments find a counterpart in the construction of a jacket. It is based on my classroom experiences of students' difficulties when tailoring garments from commercial patterns.

Grasp any opportunity of watching tailors at work in their workshops, for example at exhibitions where the craft is demonstrated. Likewise, much can be learnt by unpicking and lifting back the lining of a tailor-made jacket. I have unpicked many a lining to see what goes on inside a garment and have spent many happy hours sitting cross-legged with tailors and embroiderers in the spicy-smelling souks of Marrakesh where our common language was the craft itself.

This book sets out to show techniques of tailoring essential to a successful result. But cutting out, sewing, pressing and fitting are all involved in constructing your tailored garment. Much useful advice, which lack of space prevents my including here, is given in the companion volumes in this series.

Phase 1

Equipment

Tailoring equipment differs very little from that used in dress-making. Every creative person knows that tools themselves can be inspirational and there can't be any better motivation than having the right tools in the right place at the right time. Keep them out of sight of the family—I for one would not like my shears used for cutting off bacon rinds.

Use the equipment mentioned here for a professional approach to tailoring.

Hand-sewing needles

Various hand-sewing needles are used in stitchery. Like other sewers tailors prefer sewing needles that suit their work.

BETWEENS

Between needles are short.

Use them for short neat stitches such as decorative hand-sewn top-stitching, overcasting (oversewing), cross stitching (her-ringbone stitch) and hand-sewn twist button-holes.

Sizes most commonly used are: 6s, 7s, 8s and 9s.

SHARPS

Sharps are longer than betweens.

Use them for longer stitches such as basting, tacking, tailor's tacking and thread-marking stitches.

Sizes most commonly used are: 6s, 7s, 8s, 9s and 10s.

Tailor's tip 1

For easier threading, when sewing with double thread, use embroiderer's crewel needles; they are similar in length and size to sharps, but have longer eyes.

Note The larger the number the finer the needle.

Sewing-machine needles

Sewing-machine needles used in tailoring are generally thicker than those used in dressmaking but their points should be just as sharp. Machine stitching some man-made fabrics can blunt sewing-machine needles very rapidly, so inspect the point regularly and change the needle when blunt.

TAILORING UNUSUAL FABRICS

When tailoring unusual fabrics consult Stage 2 in the Making Clothes series, *The Sewing Machine*, a knowledgeable sales assistant, or your sewing-machine manual, on the size and type of sewing-machine needle suitable for the purpose.

Note   With sewing-machine needles the larger the number the thicker the needle.

Sizes most commonly used are 90/14s and 100/16s.

Tacking threads

Soft cotton thread sold on spools of 1000 m/1094 yds in sizes 40 and 50 is essential for thread marking. The stitches made in this soft thread cling to the fabric whereas harder sewing threads do not. White will show up on most fabrics, even on white fabrics, but a second spool of yellow, pink or blue is useful when marking distinctive alteration lines.

Note   A smaller number denotes a thicker thread.

Tailor's tip 2

To prevent your spool of soft cotton thread rolling off the table place it on the floor and squash it by standing on it.

Tailor's tip 3

Look out for large cone-shaped spools of thread often sold cheaply at markets. Use these for tacking jobs that don't require soft cotton thread.

Tailor's thimble

A tailor's thimble or shield helps prevent a sore finger at the end of a day's work and makes for a more efficient, speedier and neater method of working.

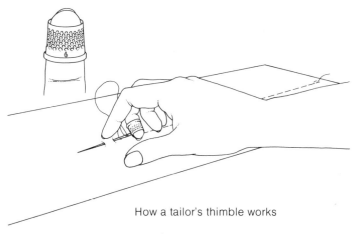

How a tailor's thimble works

Figure 1

Hand-sewing threads

In tailoring much concealed hand-stitching is worked on the right side of the garment. The thread used must not be too resilient or it will bounce back and show once the stitches are placed. For this reason pure silk thread was used for most hand-sewing in the past, but nowadays, apart from a few basic colours, it is not easily obtainable. However, most fabrics suitable for tailoring respond very well to the mercerized sewing thread sold nationwide and can quite often be machine stitched with the same thread. Alternatively choose a small reel of mercerized thread for hand sewing and a second reel of sewing-machine thread of the type recommended by the fabric manufacturers.

Bees-wax

A small block or round of bees-wax is used to make thread tangle-free, stronger and more resilient.

1 Draw the thread from the reel between your thumb and the block of bees-wax, slightly coating the thread with a fine smear of wax.

2 Smooth out the thread between your thumb and fingertip, thread your needle and, finally, cut the thread from the reel.

Dressmaker's pins

Long dressmaker's pins are as essential in tailoring as they are in dressmaking and should be clean and sharp. Throw away any that show signs of rust or they will quickly contaminate the clean pins and can permanently mark your fabric. Leave some out to work with and store the remainder in their box.

Scissors

SHEARS

Cutting-out shears with 20 to 23 cm (8 to 9 in) blades should be the best you can afford and should be kept in tip-top condition. Hairdressers would not be popular if they used blunt scissors on their clients' hair. Similarly, fabric will not respond well to blunt shears. Ask your hairdresser where he sends his scissors to be sharpened.

SMALL CUTS

Small cuts with 10 to 15 cm (4 to 6 in) blades, as their name implies, are used for smaller operations than cutting out.
Use them to clip into corners, trim seams, unpick seams and tacks, snip threads etc. Hang them round your neck on a long loop of tape for easy accessibility.

Tailor's tip 4

Choose a pair of shears or scissors thoughtfully. Used with care they will last for many years. Take some samples of fabric with you and try the scissors out on them before buying a pair. The following points will help you in making your choice:
1   They should fit your hand comfortably and cut evenly along the blades.
2   They should cut as well at the points as they cut along their length.
3   They should not bend or twist when cutting thick fabric.

PAPER-CUTTING SCISSORS

Neither the shears nor small cuts should be used for cutting paper as it takes the edge off the blade. A pair of old scissors that are easy to handle will serve this purpose very well.

10

Tailor's tip 5

To revive paper-cutting scissors cut through a piece of emery cloth or fine sandpaper for an instant sharp edge.

LEFT-HANDED SCISSORS

Scissors of all types for left-handed people can be bought from Anything Left-handed in Beak Street, London W1.

Tailor's chalk

Tailor's chalk is sold in square- or triangle-shaped pieces in various colours. *White* tailor's chalk marks most fabrics temporarily. To use efficiently always keep one edge knife sharp. To erase, lightly bang out the mark with the flat of your hand or between both hands as if applauding.

Coloured tailor's chalk is very tempting to use when marking pale coloured fabrics because one sees the mark so clearly. BEWARE—the chalk 'bangs out', but the dye in the chalk does not. Use it only for marking interfacings and calico patterns.

Note Tailor's chalk may not mark clearly after a while even though its edge appears to be sharp. Scrape over the sharp edge to remove the natural surface oil the chalk has picked up from the fabric.

Wax chalk

This chalk-like square of white or coloured wax can be used in a similar way to tailor's chalk. It clings more securely to most cloths and usually remains visible until removed by pressing with a heated iron. With coloured wax, as with coloured tailor's chalk, the wax disappears but the dye in it does not.

Tailor's tip 6

Save your thin slivers of toilet soap; they can be used in a similar manner to wax chalk.

Tracing wheel

A tracing wheel has a spiked or serrated edge.

Use on its own to prick-mark pattern lines through the pattern section you wish to copy on to copying paper placed under the pattern. Use with dressmaker's carbon tracing paper to transfer sewing and placement lines on to some fabrics. This method is especially useful when marking interfacing fabric.

11

Dressmaker's carbon tracing paper

Dressmaker's carbon tracing paper is sold in packets of assorted colours and has helpful hints on its usage on the cover. Choose a colour that stands out and yet will merge in to the seams when sewn. I find yellow carbon seems to suit most colours of fabric; it quite often shows up even on yellow fabric. Avoid bright-coloured carbon on thin or pale fabrics.

Pencils

Soft-lead HB pencils are also useful for marking sewing lines on some fabrics, interfacing and paper patterns. Avoid hard-lead pencils as their points can easily tear patterns.

Pens

Quick-drying fine-point felt-tip pens sometimes called note-takers or colour pens can be used to mark patterns and interfacings. Avoid ball-point pens as the points easily tear patterns and the ink in them can smudge on fabric.

Note Always replace the caps on pens when not in use to prevent them leaking and staining your fabric.

Pattern-making paper

Kitchen greaseproof paper sold in sheets or on a convenient roll makes sturdy paper patterns. Lay a piece over the pattern section you wish to copy or alter and trace the pattern marks on to the greaseproof paper.

Pressing equipment

IRON

Steam irons, which do not allow you to control the amount or direction of the steam, are excellent for ironing, but not suitable for pressing. A domestic iron—the best you can afford—weighing about 2 kg ($4\frac{1}{2}$ lb) and fitted with a thermostat control will enable you to press all your work to a high standard when used in conjunction with the press aids listed below.

12

PRESS BOARD

You can make a press board from 2.5 cm (1 in) thick blockboard measuring approximately 1 m × 1 m (36 × 36 in). An old, folded blanket will make an excellent pressing surface.
Use on top of a table to give a firm surface for pressing large areas.

PRESSING CLOTHS

A damp rag—a linen tea cloth will do.
Use for damp pressing.
Dry press cloths:
1   A piece of woollen worsted.
Use to firm an area after damp pressing.
2   A piece of pure silk or cotton twill.
Use to protect fabric when dry pressing.

A DABBER (Figure 2)

A dabber is a cigar-shaped tube of absorbent cloth rolled and sewn to form a 2.5 cm (1 in) thick tube.
Use to 'dab' moisture on seams, darts and difficult-to-get-at areas when pressing on the wrong side of the garment with a bare iron.

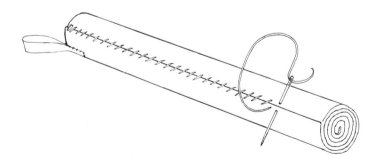

Figure 2

13

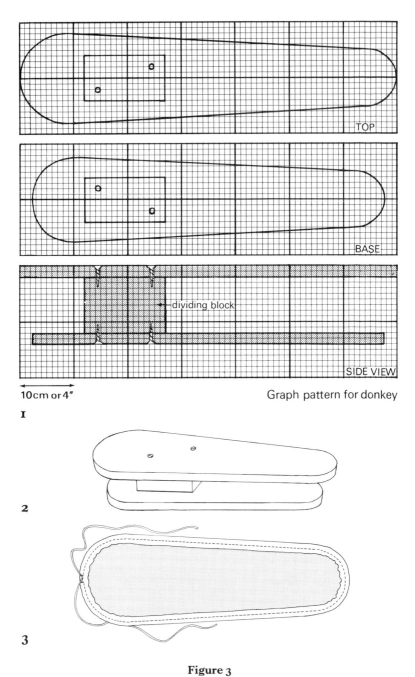

1

10cm or 4"

Graph pattern for donkey

2

3

Figure 3

14

Tailor's donkey (Figure 3)

Sometimes called a duplex board, this is an oblong, raised board. **Use** on top of the press board as a miniature ironing board.

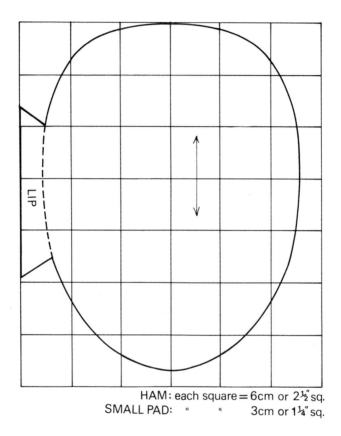

HAM: each square = 6cm or 2½″ sq.
SMALL PAD: "   "   3cm or 1¼″ sq.

Figure 4

Tailor's ham (Figure 4)

This is a firm—not hard—egg-shaped pad stuffed with chopped rags or rags and kapok.
Use when pressing, moulding and shrinking darts and fullness in dart and sleeve areas, and on top of the donkey for raising and isolating parts to be pressed.

15

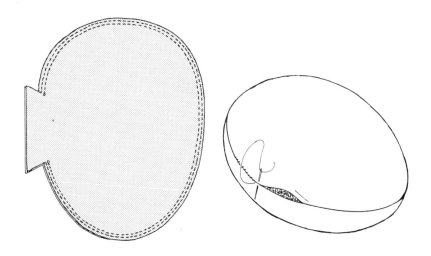

Figure 5

PRESS PAD

A press pad is a half-sized version of the tailor's ham which is used in the hand when pressing inside small or difficult-to-get-at areas.

PRESS ROLL (Figure 6)

This can be made from a stout cardboard roll, an old wooden rolling pin or a half-used roll of wallpaper, covered with a closely fitting tube of woollen worsted.

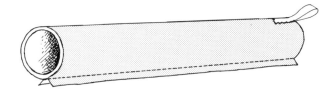

Figure 6

Use on top of the donkey when pressing seams open to prevent seam impressions showing through to the right side of the garment.

BANGER

This is a smoothly finished block of hardwood, about 8 × 8 × 18 cm (3 × 3 × 7 in).
Use to flatten the hems and edges of garments whilst still warm from the iron.

DOWEL ROD

This is a wooden curtain rail—with ends well smoothed—approximately 12 mm ($\frac{1}{2}$ in) in diameter and 50 cm (19 in) long.
Use for threading through narrow tubes of fabric for belts and rouleau when pressing open the seam.

A large wooden knitting needle can be used in the same way for smaller tubes of fabric, for getting into difficult corners (on collars, lapels etc.) and for easing out corners when turning.

Phase 2

Choice—fabrics, patterns, linings and interfacings

One has to start somewhere and, rather like the chicken and the egg, it is difficult to decide which comes first, the cloth or the style? Of course, the decision may have been made for you; you may already have a paper pattern or length of cloth stored away and you only have to find just the right fabric or style to make it in.

Tailoring can be practised on a wide range of fabrics; some of course respond more readily to the craft than others. The success of your garment will depend on how well you have chosen the cloth and the pattern. If these are your early days of tailoring do not choose a complicated paper pattern or difficult checked material and please do not make the mistake of choosing an indifferent fabric for fear of spoiling an expensive one. You are more likely to spoil an inferior fabric and in the end all the hard work you put into making it up will not be worth the effort. Do ask the advice of a knowledgeable assistant some have been in the tailoring trade themselves and can often give advice on which fabrics and paper patterns make up well. Paper pattern envelopes usually give good suggestions on types of fabric to use, and pattern catalogues often have photographs of the garment made up in a suitable fabric.

Fabrics
Tailoring fabrics divide easily into four categories:
1 Plain fabrics without nap. These are simplest to use as they can be cut up or down the fabric.
2 Plain fabrics with nap. These require all the pattern pieces to be cut in one direction.
3 Patterned fabrics with both-way design. These can be cut up or down the fabric.

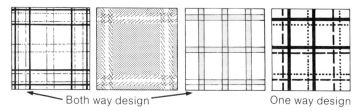

Both way design — One way design

Figure 7

4 Patterned fabrics with one-way design. These require all pattern pieces to be cut in one direction.

Note Fabrics that need to be cut in one direction usually need more cloth.

Patterns

Classic styles make up well in any of the materials mentioned above. Designer garments often incorporate the simplicity of cut of classic styles and yet perhaps introduce an interesting shaped yoke, or clever seam detail. A plain fabric will show off these details better.

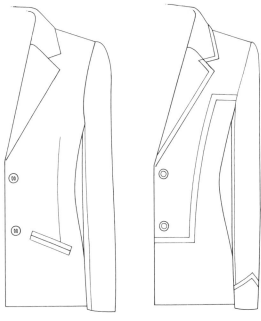

A classic jacket   A designer jacket

Figure 8

19

Tailor's tip 7

Measuring up for fabric quantities.

1   Using the edge of a table as a guide, measure in half the width of the material you wish to buy and lay a piece of string along it. For example if the material is 90 cm (36 in) wide lay the string 45 cm (18 in) from the edge of the table.

2   Place your pattern pieces on this imaginary lay to find out how much cloth you need.

3   Make a rough sketch of the pattern positions and mark fold and selvedge.

Linings

COLOUR

Should you be unable to match a lining colour to your fabric choose a complementary colour. An attractive lining should be a hidden glory and, in a coat or jacket, can give you pleasure each time you take the garment off. Near misses in colour matching offend the eye, whereas a tone can complement the colour of your fabric. Base your choice of lining colour on the predominant colour of your fabric.

Browns   Choose the paler beiges or darker shades in the same tone range.

Greys   Choose silver for medium grey, black for clerical grey.

Blues   Choose pale or medium blues in the same tone range.

Or choose a complete contrast : black with red ; orange with brown ; emerald green with black.

Tailor's tip 8

The wide range of colours on a decorator's sample card will give you lots of colour contrast ideas.

QUALITY

Do not make the mistake of choosing a poor-quality lining, it will not wear well and relining a garment is a tedious business. Choose a lining that is soft and will slip easily over woollen jumpers. A stiff lining can often make a jacket bounce out in the strangest places.

QUANTITY

This book uses the garment as a lining pattern and so the quantities given here may differ from those on the pattern envelope. It is a good idea to measure the pattern pieces using Tailor's tip 7.

Interfacings

Interfacing shapes vary from pattern to pattern but their purpose remains the same: to enhance and give substance to the garment, allowing it to flow flatteringly over the body, and to help prevent hems and edges from stretching.

Tailors have their own favourite interfacings, usually those that suit most garments. Keep your choice to a minimum. I favour the following:

TAILOR'S CANVAS—UNBLEACHED

Tailor's canvas (sometimes called holland or shrunk duck) is used for the fronts and under collar sections.

Note Despite its name, this fabric shrinks.

DRESSMAKER'S CALICO—UNBLEACHED

Medium-weight dressmaker's calico is used for interfacing hems of jackets and sleeves. It is usually cut on the bias.

DOMETTE—BLACK OR WHITE

Knitted fleecy domette, (sometimes called lambswool or Eskimo) is used for bumping out sleeve heads.

SEAM RIBBON BINDING—BLACK OR WHITE

Seam ribbon binding (sometimes called lute ribbon) is used for taping lapel crease lines and front edges.

Tailor's tip 9

Keep the off-cuts of all interfacings in a bit bag, the small pieces can be very useful for minor interfaced sections.

Quantities

TAILOR'S CANVAS

One and a half times the length of the front of the garment will give you ample interfacing for the fronts, back armhole and under collar sections.

CALICO

70 cm ($\frac{3}{4}$ yd) will be enough to provide unjoined bias strips for the hem-lines of the garment.

DOMETTE

A small quantity, say 30 cm (12 in) per garment, should be enough for filling out sleeve heads. Choose white for all but darker coloured fabrics.

SEAM RIBBON BINDING

One metre is ample for most lapel crease lines. You will need more if you wish to tape the front edges.

Tailor's tip 10

When tailoring white or pale fabrics choose white interfacings, as the unbleached shade of most canvases will show through and give your garment a dingy look. Interfacings similar to the unbleached variety are available in white.

Phase 3

Patterns

Proving the pattern

Cut out all the pattern pieces relevant to the garment you are making and pin them together to prove to yourself that the garment actually fits together. Problems can often be solved at this stage by reading the assembly instruction sheet as you proceed, noting the points that may be confusing or need extra care. Should the pattern appear not to fit together make sure that you have not missed pinning a dart, overlooked ease or fullness incorporated into the pattern, or left out one of the smaller pattern pieces such as a side body, under sleeve or yoke section. It is a good idea to count those pattern pieces that make up the main body of the garment and make a note of them.

Note   All other pattern pieces are additions to the main body, a facing covers a lapel, a top collar covers an under collar etc.

PATTERN TRY ON

A number of uncertainties can be eliminated at this stage thus paving the way to a more successful first fitting.

Body section

Pin together the body sections of the pattern with the seam allowances on the outside so that you have a sleeveless, collarless, inside-out half shell. Carefully slide the shell on to your body to observe and note whether:

1   The bust position is correct.
2   The waist length is correct.

Make any adjustment before observing and noting whether:

3   The hip of the jacket is too small, or too large.
4   The length of the jacket is suitable.

Figure 9

24

Sleeve

Pin together the sleeve pattern in a similar manner and slide it on to your arm positioning the crown of the sleeve to a suitable shoulder width and observe and note whether:

1 The sleeve is large enough around the top arm.
2 The elbow dart or seam fits into place.
3 The sleeve length is suitable.

Note This stage will give you a general idea of the fit of the garment, what minor adjustments you can make to the pattern and what extra seam and hem allowances you may find useful when fitting the actual garment.

Special note Patterns without seam allowances can be tried on in a similar manner. Pin together the pattern pieces 3 mm ($\frac{1}{8}$ in) from the sewing line remembering to make allowances for the extra when estimating the fit.

Example Bust darts, waistlines and hem-lines will all be 3 mm ($\frac{1}{8}$ in) higher than they should be because you have pinned up the shoulder line 3 mm ($\frac{1}{8}$ in) higher than it should be.

Tailor's tip 11
Underline or mark your observations, unusual pattern instructions such as ease, stretch, clip to here etc. on the pattern piece and instruction sheet with a distinctive coloured note-taker pen so that these important points of assembly are easily recognized.

Tailors's tip 12
For easy accessibility, instant recognition and to lessen the risk of torn patterns, slit open the bottom and right-hand edges of the pattern envelope and insert it, face upwards, in an A4 or foolscap transparent folder obtainable from office stationers. This larger container will accommodate your pattern pieces more readily and the plain side of the pattern envelope can be used for notes and remarks. Other pattern pieces not needed for your chosen style are best kept under separate cover, but remember to label them.

Multi-size patterns

Multi-size patterns are now marketed by many pattern companies and are good value if you wish to make up the garment in several sizes or can share the pattern with friends. At first sight they can be confusing, with so many lines on them they appear to resemble an aerial view of a railway terminus. Study one of the smaller pattern pieces carefully whilst reading the instructions relating to this particular aspect and you will notice that each size has a different type of line. These different lines range from a squiggle to a dot and dash.

MULTI-SIZE PATTERNS WITH SEAM ALLOWANCES

Multi-size patterns with seam allowances sometimes have both sewing and cutting lines marked on them. Should you wish to cut one size only from the pattern concentrate on the line-type depicting the cutting line for your chosen size and carefully cut around all the pattern pieces on that line.

MULTI-SIZE PATTERNS WITHOUT SEAM ALLOWANCES (Figure 10)

Multi-size patterns without seam allowances are quite popular nowadays. Usually printed on a heavier paper than the usual pattern paper tissue, they have only one line-type per size, the sewing line. Cut around the pattern pieces on the line-type depicting your size, and constantly remind yourself that seam allowances must be added when cutting out your fabric.

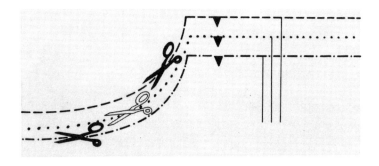

Figure 10

Tailor's tip 13

To avoid confusion, mark over the line-type for your size with a distinctive coloured pen choosing a second colour for the cutting line if it is included in the pattern. Do not attempt laboriously to mark the pattern in a continuous line but make a series of dots or dashes along the chosen lines sufficient to make them stand out from all the other lines.

Pattern conservation

Apart from the obvious desirability of being able to share your pattern or make it up in various sizes it is helpful when tailoring to have a sturdy paper pattern to work from. So make a copy of the size you want.

1 Working on a large enough surface smooth out the section of pattern you wish to copy. Place a piece of greaseproof paper over it and pin the two together.

2 Trace the pattern lines and symbols clearly visible through the greaseproof paper onto the greaseproof paper using a soft lead pencil.

3 Before removing the pins and cutting out your greaseproof paper pattern check carefully that you have marked all lines, symbols etc. onto it.

Note Seam allowances can be added or omitted; the choice is yours.

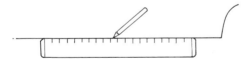

Figure 11

Tailor's tip 14 (Figures 11 and 12)

Trace the straight lines with the help of a ruler held steady against them.

27

Trace curves in a series of dashes by resting the heel of your hand on the table and using it as a pivot point.

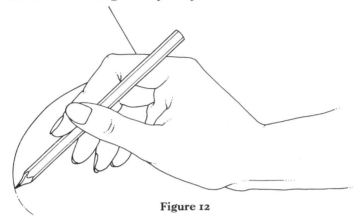

Figure 12

Tailor's tip 15

To mend or strengthen a torn or weak section of pattern:

1 Cut a patch of paper of similar weight to that of the pattern and smooth a few strokes of stick glue over the patch.

2 Position and smooth down one edge of the tear on to the patch then position and smooth down the other edge of the tear to meet it.

3 Trim away any excess paper from the patch.

Mixing pattern sizes

Mixing pattern sizes is possible with a little thought and care, the obvious liaison being a larger skirt size to that of a jacket.

LARGE UPPER ARM

Use a larger size sleeve pattern and hollow out bodice underarm.

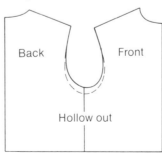

Figure 13

Use a larger size front and sleeve pattern and hollow out back underarm, reshape front shoulder.

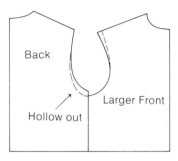

Figure 14

Alterations to paper patterns

Alteration to paper patterns is outside the scope of this book, but is explained in the companion Making Clothes book on *Fitting*.

Phase 4

Cutting out

Laying out fabric

SURFACE INSPECTION

Be sure to check the surface of your cloth for damage or flaws. The right side of the cloth is all important and should be held up to a good light source for close inspection. What may appear to be flaws on the wrong side of the fabric could easily be thread joinings. They do not show up on the right side of the fabric and should be ignored. Tack mark around any damaged or flawed area so that you can easily recognize and avoid it when laying the pattern on and cutting out on the wrong side of the fabric.

Note   Should the damage be on the underside of the folded fabric when laid out, mark its position with a safety pin on the layer above it.

OFF-GRAIN TWIST (Figures 15 and 16)

Even the best of fabrics can be rolled or baled out of true with the straight grain and will not lay flat when laid out on the fold. Unless the twist is straightened before cutting out, the pattern pieces on one side of the garment will hang differently to those on the other side and the garment will not balance.

CHECKING FOR OFF-GRAIN TWIST (Figures 15 and 16)

1   Make sure that one end of the length of fabric is cut or torn on the across grain. If not, draw a thread along the width of the piece.
2   Fold the fabric in half lengthways.
3   With both hands grasp the fold edge at the straightened end and gently shake it.
4   As if laying a table cloth, lay the folded length down on to the cutting surface using the edge of the cutting table as a guide.
5   The torn or grain cut edges of the folded fabric should fall naturally together and the whole folded length lie smoothly over the cutting surface.

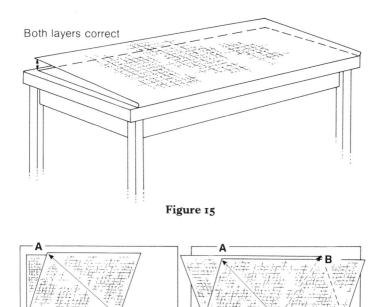

Both layers correct

Figure 15

A
B
One (upper) layer twisted
A
B
Both layers twisted

Rectification: tug of war corner A versus corner B with the help of a friend pull the length of cloth on the bias. Stretch from A – B to untwist.

Figure 16

Tailor's tip 16

Before purchasing a length of fabric, check it for flaws or damage (red tape or string threaded through the selvedge often denotes damage in that area). Be sure to ask the sales assistant to cut or tear the length of cloth on the across grain, which is the true weave of the fabric from selvedge to selvedge.

If uncertain, ask the assistant to point out the right side of the fabric so that you can mark it with a safety pin.

Tailor's tip 17

Fabrics that have been stored for some time can look crumbled and careworn. Hang the length of cloth over the top of an open door for a day or so and most, if not all of its creases will fall out.

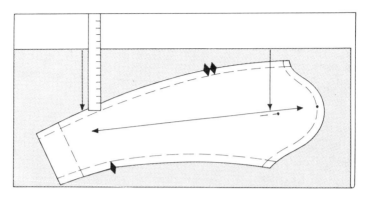

Figure 17

Laying on the pattern

Rehearse the pattern instruction sheet layout guide by placing all the pattern pieces required, unpinned, on to the cloth. Place the large pieces first, medium second and finally fill in with the small pieces. Small weights such as pin boxes and scissors will help to keep them in position.

GRAIN CHECK (Figure 17)

If the pattern pieces are not positioned accurately on the grain of the fabric, the garment will hang badly. Using a ruler and the selvedge or fold edge as a guide, correctly position the pattern pieces starting with the larger pieces.

1 Place one pin through the grain line at the widest part of the pattern piece.

2 Using a ruler, measure the distance from the pin to the nearest edge (fold or selvedge) and note this measurement.

3 Set the ruler at the same distance from the edge further along the pattern at the other end of the grain line.

4 Swing or pivot the pattern piece to line up with the ruler and place a second pin at that point.

Your pattern piece is now laid accurately on grain. Continue pinning on your pattern pieces in a similar manner until they are all positioned and then use extra pins to hold the pattern pieces in place.

Note Pattern pieces placed on a fold are naturally positioned along the grain.

Special note Remember to leave room for seam allowances for patterns that don't have them.

Cutting out

Once you have established that all the pattern pieces are correctly placed you are ready to cut them out. At this stage, and especially if you are using the floor as a cutting surface, the strain on your back, eyes and need I say nerves is very great if you try to cut out the pieces slavishly following the exact cutting edges. An easier way is to cut through the spaces around the larger pattern pieces, thus separating them into more manageable areas and then trim around the cutting line. On patterns without seam allowances, you can add the cutting line at a more convenient level.

Phase 5

Marking techniques

Much of the inside of a tailored garment is covered by interfacing that will eventually hide many of the sewing and placement lines if they are marked only on the wrong side of the garment. The little time spent in thread marking the sewing and placement lines will save a great deal of effort wasted by constantly searching for or referring to, the pattern for lost or hidden lines, balance marks and symbols.

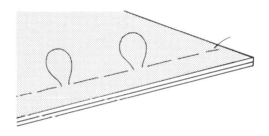

Figure 18

Thread marking—close version (Figure 18)

Use for marking areas where intricate shapes, such as necklines, armholes, curved seam lines etc. need to be clearly defined.

1 Thread a needle with soft cotton thread and make two running stitches through both layers of cloth at one end of the line to be marked.

2 Re-enter the needle close to the point where it last came out and make two further running stitches.

3 Pull the thread through the cloth until a small loop remains at the re-entry point.

4 Continue re-entering, making two stitches at a time and leaving small loops all along the line to be marked.

34

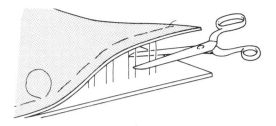

Figure 19

Separation (Figure 19)

To separate, firmly pull the two layers apart and clip the soft cotton thread between the two layers.

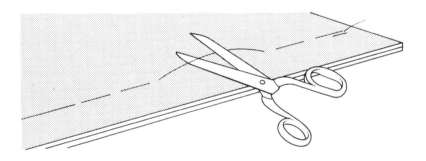

Figure 20

Thread marking—open version (Figure 20)

Use for marking long straight sewing lines, hem and placement lines.

1 Thread a needle with soft cotton thread and make two stitches through both layers of cloth.

2 Re-enter the needle approximately 5 cm (2 in) away from the last two stitches and make two further stitches.

3 Pull the thread through to lie loosely over the gap.

4 Continue re-entering making two stitches and leaving similar gaps all along the line to be marked.

To separate, snip the long stitch in half (the gap stitch) and pull the two layers of fabric slightly apart. Clip the cotton thread between the two layers.

Note These two methods allow instant recognition of the right and wrong sides of your fabric. The neat fringe effect will be the right side of the fabric and the untidier loops will be on the wrong side of the garment sections.

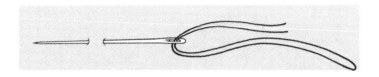

Figure 21

Tailor's tip 18 (Figure 21)

It is advisable to use double cotton thread for marking all but the thinnest of tailoring fabrics. For a knot-free and tangle-free length of cotton pass both ends of the thread through the eye of the needle leaving the loop at the other end. Try this method when hand-sewing with double thread.

Using thread marks—on patterns without seam allowances

On patterns without seam allowances simply thread mark around the edges of the pattern choosing the open or closed thread marking method as appropriate. To mark placement lines within the pattern see p. 37.

Using thread marks—on patterns with seam allowances

On patterns with seam allowances pin the pattern on to the fabric with the pins inside the sewing lines, so that the edges of the pattern can be lifted up.

1 Using a ruler for straight lines and your finger tips for curves, press the pattern piece along the sewing line onto the fabric below.

36

Figure 22a

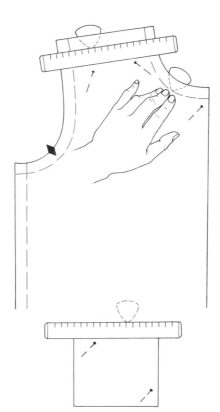

Figure 22b

2   Lift the edge of the pattern up and with a knife-edge piece of tailor's chalk mark the sewing line onto the fabric, using the edge of the ruler or finger tips as a guide.

3   Continue chalk-marking all around the pattern section and, with the pattern still pinned on but lifted up, thread mark along the chalked sewing lines.

Marking placement lines

Placement lines, darts etc. within the pattern are marked once the outer sewing lines have been thread marked.

Note   Only the main body sections need be marked in such a manner. Many of the pattern pieces are covers to the main pattern. *Example*: A top collar covers and thus takes the shape from the under collar. A facing covers and therefore takes the shape from the front section.

Phase 6

Assembly

Tailoring or 'building' a jacket is a precise and progressive craft passing through four important stages. Firstly, stage one, the basic shell or skeleton fitting is prepared and perfected ready to house the structural supporting interfacings of stage two. Finally, in stage three the lapels and under collar are covered and in stage four the lining is inserted and the button-holes made. At each stage there are decisions to be made and uncertainties to be eliminated.

Stage one—the basic shell

The basic shell or skeleton fitting is tacked together, tried on and fitted, corrected and tried on again. Once a perfect fit is obtained, any seams and darts in the back and front sections are machine sewn, then pressed so that the interfacing structure can be built into them.

Decisions to be made at this stage are shown in Figure 23.

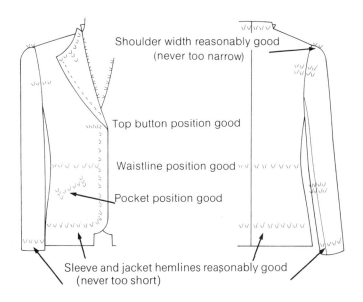

Shoulder width reasonably good
(never too narrow)

Top button position good

Waistline position good

Pocket position good

Sleeve and jacket hemlines reasonably good
(never too short)

Figure 23

Stage two—interfacing insertion

The interfacings, pockets and other bits and pieces called trim-
mings that help build a tailor-made garment can be very bewilder-
ing to a newcomer to the craft, even though a top-coat is often
only as large as a dress and a jacket similar in shape to a blouse.

Methodical tailors will often work on the back, fronts and sleeves
of a garment separately, building in the interfacings as they go,
and making the pockets and covering the lapels before finally join-
ing the back to the fronts. This method reduces the bulk of the
garment you have to work with and ends the constant search for
that part you wish to work on.

Tailor's tip 19

For a crease-free garment, pin the sections you are not working
on to a padded coat-hanger so that they can be hung up out of
the way.

39

INTERFACINGS

Interfacings can be cut directly from the pattern sections if no
separate pattern is provided. It is a good idea to cut your own
interfacing pattern by tracing off the areas to be interfaced as
shown in Figure 11 using greaseproof paper as in the method
described for pattern conservation p. 27.

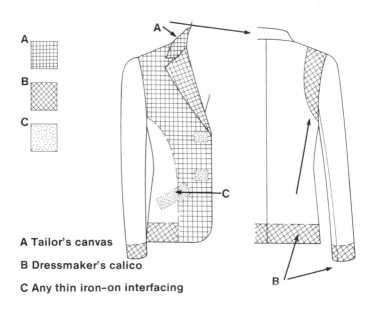

A Tailor's canvas

B Dressmaker's calico

C Any thin iron–on interfacing

Right side of jacket with shaded interfaced areas

Figure 24

SHRINKING INTERFACINGS

It is essential to shrink interfacings cut from tailor's canvas and
calico. This is done by pressing the interfacing with a hot iron
under a damp press cloth until it and the press cloth are dry.

FRONT INTERFACINGS

Using a soft-lead pencil or note-taker pen lightly, but clearly, mark
the lapel roll-line, front edge line and front waist mark on the
interfacing.

40

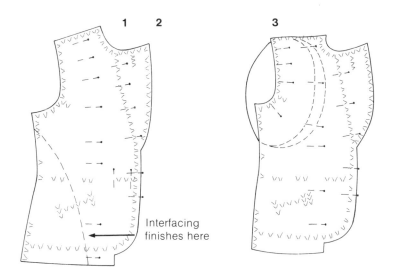

Figure 25

Positioning the fronts

Position the front interfacings by pinning the wrong side of the outside of the jacket on to the interfacing (Figure 25).

1 Working on a flat surface pin the jacket fronts to the interfacings, matching the lapel roll-lines, front edges and waist marks.

2 Smooth out the fronts over the interfacing and place pins down the centre of the jacket fronts to hold the two layers together.

3 Working over a tailor's ham as if it were a side body, mould each side of the jacket over the interfacing and place further pins to hold the two layers together at the shoulder and armhole seamlines.

Fixing

Fix the fabric to the interfacing by tack stitching through both layers all along the sewing lines. The lapel roll-line, front edge, waist mark, shoulder line and armhole line should be clearly visible on the interfaced side of each front so tack with a distinctive coloured thread.

41

Stay tape the lapel roll-line using well-shrunk seam ribbon binding to prevent lapel sag (Figure 26).

Positioning

Position the tape along the inside edge of the lapel roll-line and pin it in place.

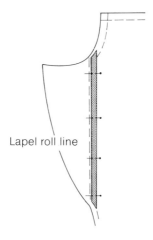

Lapel roll line

Figure 26

Fixing

Tack along both edges of the tape to fix it.

Under collar interfacing

The under collar interfacing is cut on the same grain as the under collar itself.

Fixing (Figure 27)

1 Join the centre-back seam flat and trim away excess seam allowance.
2 Pin the under collar to the interfacing and tack stitch through the roll-line to hold the two layers together.

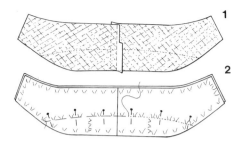

Figure 27

BACK ARMHOLE INTERFACING

The back armhole interfacings are cut on the opposite grain to the back armhole. This prevents back underarm stretch and provides a mini shoulder pad or shelf for sleeves, or shoulder pads if used, to rest on.

Positioning and fixing
See Figure 28a.

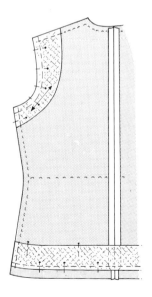

Figure 28a

43

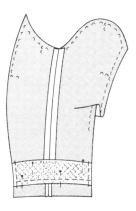

Figure 28b

HEM AND SLEEVE-HEM INTERFACINGS

Hem and sleeve-hem interfacings are cut from bias strips of calico 12 cms ($4\frac{1}{2}$ in) wide and long enough for each section.

Positioning and fixing

See Figure 28b.

Note   Should the hem-line be curved, with a hot iron stretch or shape the bias strip to match the curve before positioning it.

POCKET REINFORCEMENT (Figure 29)

Pocket openings that are cut into the garment itself need reinforcing with strips of interfacing before they are sewn and cut open. Strips of woven iron-on interfacing carefully pressed in place will help prevent the cut and clipped pocket openings from fraying.

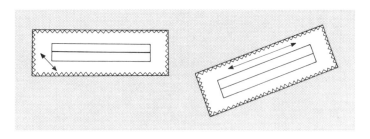

Figure 29

For extra strength cut the interfacing strips on the opposite grain to the pocket opening.

It is a good idea to press smaller patches of this interfacing over the button-hole positions for extra strength.

Tailor's tip 20

To help prevent the impression of fusible (iron-on) interfacings from showing on the right side of the garment serrate the edges of the reinforcement strips with pinking shears before pressing them in place.

Now that all interfacings are in position and the garment has progressed a stage further, carefully tack the side seams and shoulder seams together and tack up the hems, front and lapel edges. Try the garment on and make any necessary corrections.

Tailor's tip 21

To help visualize the finished garment pin on button-size circles and pocket shapes cut from the fabric scraps.

Stage three—covering the interfacing

Before the interfacing can be covered with hems, lapel facings and top collar, the pad stitching and catch stitching must be done to help keep the garment's shape during its lifetime (Figures 30 and 31).

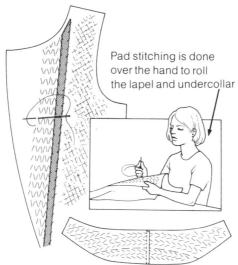

Pad stitching is done over the hand to roll the lapel and undercollar

Figure 30

45

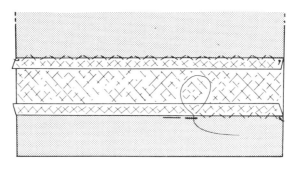

Catch stitch along the fold edge
to prevent becoming dislodged in wear

Figure 31

POCKETS

Pockets can be made at an earlier stage if you are sure of their positions but if made at this stage the canvas must be lifted back so that the machine stitching and cutting is done only through the strips of interfacing reinforcement.

Jetted pocket

Making the jets (Figure 32)

1   Cut two strips of fabric (jets) for each pocket, 5 cm (2 in) longer than the pocket length and 5 cm (2 in) deeper than the chosen jet width.

2   Baste the strips into position and chalk-mark stitching lines on them the chosen width of the jets.

3   Machine stitch along these lines starting and finishing off firmly and exactly at each pocket end.

4   Cut along the pocket mouth and clip in to the corners close to the machine stitching.

5   Trim away a small amount from the cut pocket mouth to allow room when folding the jets over the seams.

6   Pull the jets through the pocket mouth and arrange them so that they meet to cover the pocket opening.

7   Turn in the clipped corners and secure with stab-stitching. Stab-stitch the arranged jets into position concealing the stitch in the seam.

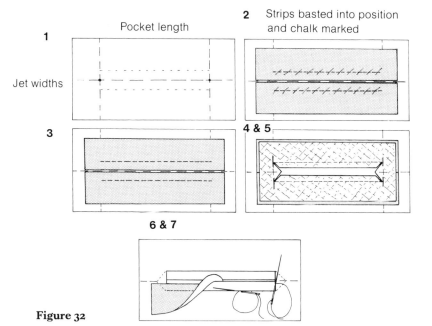

Figure 32

Making the pocket bag (Figure 33)

1 For each pocket cut a piece of lining as wide as the jets and deep enough for a pocket. Join this to the lower jet.

2 Cut a piece of the garment fabric the same width as the jets and as deep as the jets plus the joined-on lining.

3 Position this over the jets and lining and machine stitch it to the lined jets to complete the pocket.

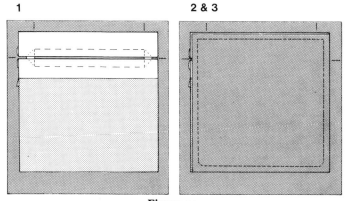

Figure 33

47

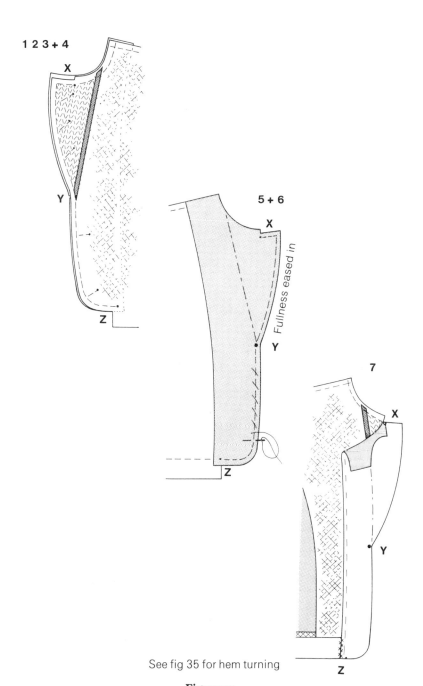

1 2 3 + 4

5 + 6

Fullness eased in

7

See fig 35 for hem turning

Figure 34

48

1 Press the pad-stitched lapels flat to make the stitches sink into the interfacing.

2 Tack mark the lapel shape in a distinctive colour through to the interfaced sides and clearly mark points X, Y and Z.

3 Lay the fronts over the facings, right sides together, and secure with a few pins.

4 Trim away the seam allowances to all but 10 mm ($\frac{3}{8}$ in) on the front edges and lapel shapes, leaving a little extra—say 3 mm ($\frac{1}{8}$ in) on the lapel facing.

5 Working from the facing side ease the extra fullness on to the lapel shape and baste the fronts into position.

6 Machine stitch from the interfacing side between Z and X using the distinctive tack marking as a sewing guide.

7 Remove tacks, trim away (layer) the edges, turn and baste edges into position and catch-stitch to the interfacing.

Special note Ease is approximate. Some fabrics will ease in much more readily than others.

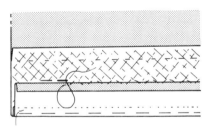

Catch stitching sleeve
and jacket hems

Figure 35

If you have been working with each piece separate up to now tack and machine stitch the shoulders and side seams and press.

Note Interfacings are sewn into the shoulder.

TURNING UP HEMS

The hem allowance is caught to the hem interfacing only (Figure 35).

49

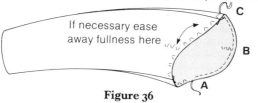

From no fullness at A a gradual build up
to most fullness at B and then gradually less to C

If necessary ease
away fullness here

C

B

A

Figure 36

SLEEVES AND UNDER COLLAR

Sleeves and under collar are tacked into position for the final
fitting. One cannot be fitted without the other as they interact.

SETTING IN SLEEVES (Figure 36)

For complete control of fullness finely hand gather along the sewing line from A to C.

Sew in sleeves either by machine or by hand, whichever you
prefer. Remove any tacks, press and bump out sleeve heads (p. 51).

Note Sleeves are sewn in through all layers, fabric and
interfacing.

SEWING ON THE UNDER COLLAR (Figure 37)

Position and pin the turned under neck edge of the under collar
on to the jacket and finely hand sew it from X to X.

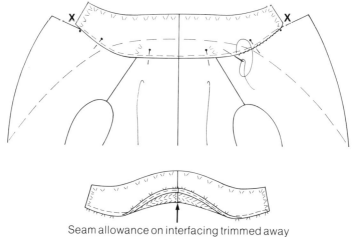

Seam allowance on interfacing trimmed away
and neck edge turned under

Figure 37

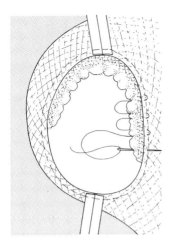

Figure 38

BUMPING OUT (Figure 38)

Bump out the sleeve heads using knitted fleecy domette.

1   Cut a strip of fleecy domette for each sleeve, approximately 25 cm (10 in) long by 16 cm (6 in) wide, folded lengthways.

2   Position the folded strip centrally over the sleeve head and fix with a few pins.

3   Working from the armhole side stitch the bump through the armhole stitching line with long tight stitches on the bump side to grip it into place.

Note   Several layers of domette can be used for fuller sleeve heads.

SHOULDER PADS

Positioning and fixing: see Figure 39

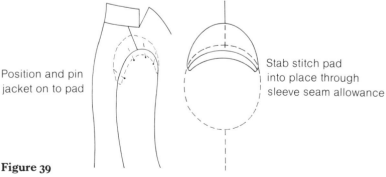

Position and pin jacket on to pad

Stab stitch pad into place through sleeve seam allowance

Figure 39

TOP COLLAR (Figure 40)

1 Press the under collar to make the stitches sink into the interfacing.

2 Clearly tack mark the under collar shape through to the interfaced side.

3 Lay the top collar, right sides together, over the under collar and position with a few pins.

4 Trim away the seam allowance to all but 10 mm ($\frac{3}{8}$ in) on the under collar, leaving a little extra on the top collar, say 3 mm ($\frac{1}{8}$ in).

5 Ease the extra fullness on to the under collar, baste into position and machine stitch using the distinctive tack mark as a sewing guide.

6 Trim away (layer) the edges, turn out to the right sides, fold in edges and hand sew as shown.

1 2 3 4 5   **6**

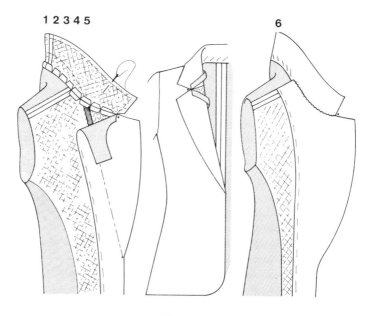

Figure 40

Stage four—finishing

It is suggested that you use the garment pattern for a more accurately fitting lining.

BODY LINING (Figure 41)

Cut the front lining as shown using the front edge as a guide line. Allow an extra 2 cm ($\frac{3}{4}$ in) on the centre back for a pleat. Stitch and tack as shown. Darts, if any, are tacked into place and can be sewn and clipped as illustrated. Leave pleat tack in position until the garment is completed.

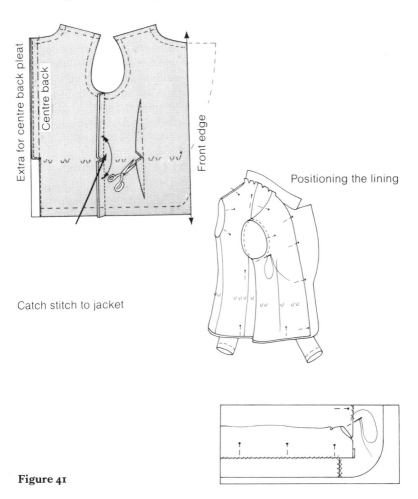

Extra for centre back pleat

Centre back

Front edge

Positioning the lining

Catch stitch to jacket

Figure 41

53

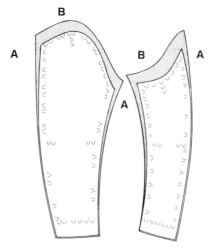

Figure 42

SLEEVE LINING (Figure 42)

Sleeve linings are made up bigger than the sleeves themselves to prevent them from splitting in wear. Allow 1 cm ($\frac{3}{8}$ in) extra at top arm seams (A) and 2 cm ($\frac{3}{4}$ in) extra on underarm and sleeve head (B).

For easier positioning turn in the sleeve head and gather stitch the crown (Figure 43).

PRESSING LINING

Do not press the seam allowances open. Press only along the unopened seams to set the stitches, clip if necessary to allow the unopened seam allowances to roll to one side when positioning the lining into the garment.

POSITIONING LINING

Position the lining with the help of the tailor's ham or donkey.

1 Position and pin the lining over the garment matching the waist marks, centre back seam, shoulders and side seams.

2 Lift back lining and loosely catch a small section of the side seam allowances to the side seams of the jacket (Figure 41). Do not attempt to turn in any edges yet but continue pinning until the whole lining is in position.

3 Catch stitch lining to armhole.

1 Turn and pin up the lining evenly to the jacket hem edge. Clip the back neck edge, turn in and pin the back neck and front edges so that they cover the top collar and facing catch stitches.

2 Pass the turned-in lining hem up 3 cm ($1\frac{1}{4}$ in) and hem stitch it to the hem allowance to form the hem pleat.

3 Allow the hem pleat to drop and hand stitch the front edges and neck into place.

SLEEVES (Figure 43)

1 Position and pin the sleeve lining to the sleeve seam, lift the lining back and loosely catch a small section of the sleeve seam allowances together.

2 Arrange the sleeve head over the armhole, draw up the gathers and hem stitch.

3 Pin up the sleeve lining hem and form a pleat similar to that on the jacket lining hem.

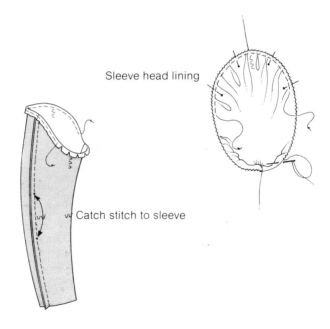

Sleeve head lining

Catch stitch to sleeve

Figure 43

55

Twist button-holes (Figure 44)

1   Mark the button-hole position and punch or cut a small hole or triangle at the front edge of the placement line.

2   Work small running stitches all around the button-hole mark and eye to keep all the layers in place.

3   From the eye end cut along the remainder of the hole and overcast the raw edges.

THE INNER CORD

Thread a needle with double, bees-waxed button-hole twist and position this inner cord along the first side of the button-hole to be worked.

THE STITCH

1   Thread a second needle with sufficient single, bees-waxed button-hole twist to complete one hole.

Example: A 2.5 cm (1 in) hole will use up approximately one metre of twist.

2   Cast on and work the stitches over the inner cord.

Points to remember:

1   Use your thumb as a stitch width guide.

2   The purl is pulled into the button-hole until you reach the eye. It is then pulled upwards around the eye and then inwards as before along the final side.

3   Remember to reposition the inner cord as you work.

4   Choose a perfect match or, if you can't find that, a slightly darker button-hole twist.

5   To help prevent the thread from gnarling, when making the stitches use the needle only to pull the twist through the fabric and your thumb and finger to position the purl.

6   Choose a needle with an eye big enough for the twist to slip through easily.

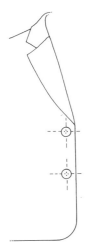

Buttonhole positions

1, 2 & 3

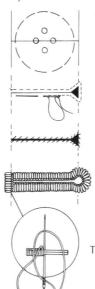

The bar

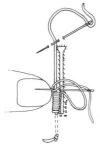

The stitch

Figure 44

57

FINISHING THE BUTTON-HOLE (Figure 45)

Insert the tip of a pencil into the eye of the button-hole and gently pull the ends of inner cord so that they slightly draw up and neaten the eye stitches around the pencil. Finally, with the remainder of the button-hole thread, work a button-holed bar along the back end of the button-hole, making sure you catch in the inner cords by stabbing them through whilst working the bar. Cut off the remainder of the inner cord.

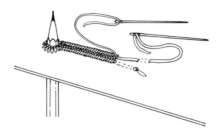

Figure 45

Variations on a theme

MAKING SHOULDER PADS (Figures 46a, b and c)

Lay the pattern piece shoulder seams together and trace off the shoulder pad as shown. Cut the shape out in stiff or double interfacing. Build up the pad shape using several graduated layers of wadding. Hold them together with large stitches.

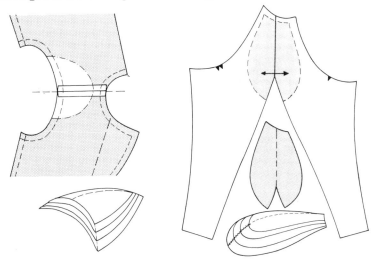

Shoulder pad for a set-in sleeve

Figure 46a

Shoulder pad for a raglan sleeve

Figure 46b

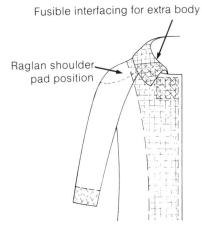

Fusible interfacing for extra body

Raglan shoulder pad position

Figure 46c

Buttons with a special finish (Figure 47)

Choose a rimmed button that will complement the colours in your tweed or check mixture.

1 Press on fusible interfacing to the wrong side of your fabric and cut out circles to fit the centre of the button.

2 Glue these circles into position.

Figure 47

Note Coins make good templates from which to cut these circles and to test whether or not they will fit.

Breast plates (Figure 48)

Breast plates are often inserted into tailored garments to help prevent the chest and shoulders from sagging. Cut them out from non-woven interfacing—felt, flannel or cotton haircloth—slash and attach them to the front interfacings with pad stitches as shown.

Note They are not sewn into the shoulder seams but are included when sewing in the sleeves.

Slash breast plate

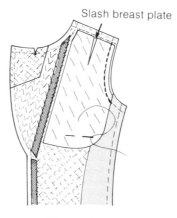

Figure 48

60

TAPING EDGES (Figure 49)

Garments made from loosely woven fabrics may need the front edges taped to prevent sagging.

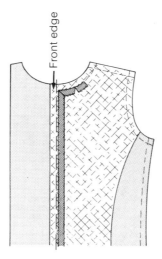

Figure 49

Note   Catch stitch the interfacing to the front edge of the garment and the pre-shrunk tape to the interfacing.

COLLAR AND LAPEL CORNERS (Figure 50)

Collar and lapel corners can be given a crisper finish by pressing pieces of fusible interfacing on to the interfacing before covering the collar and lapels.

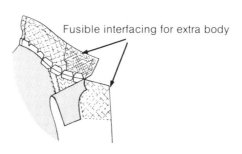

Fusible interfacing for extra body

Figure 50